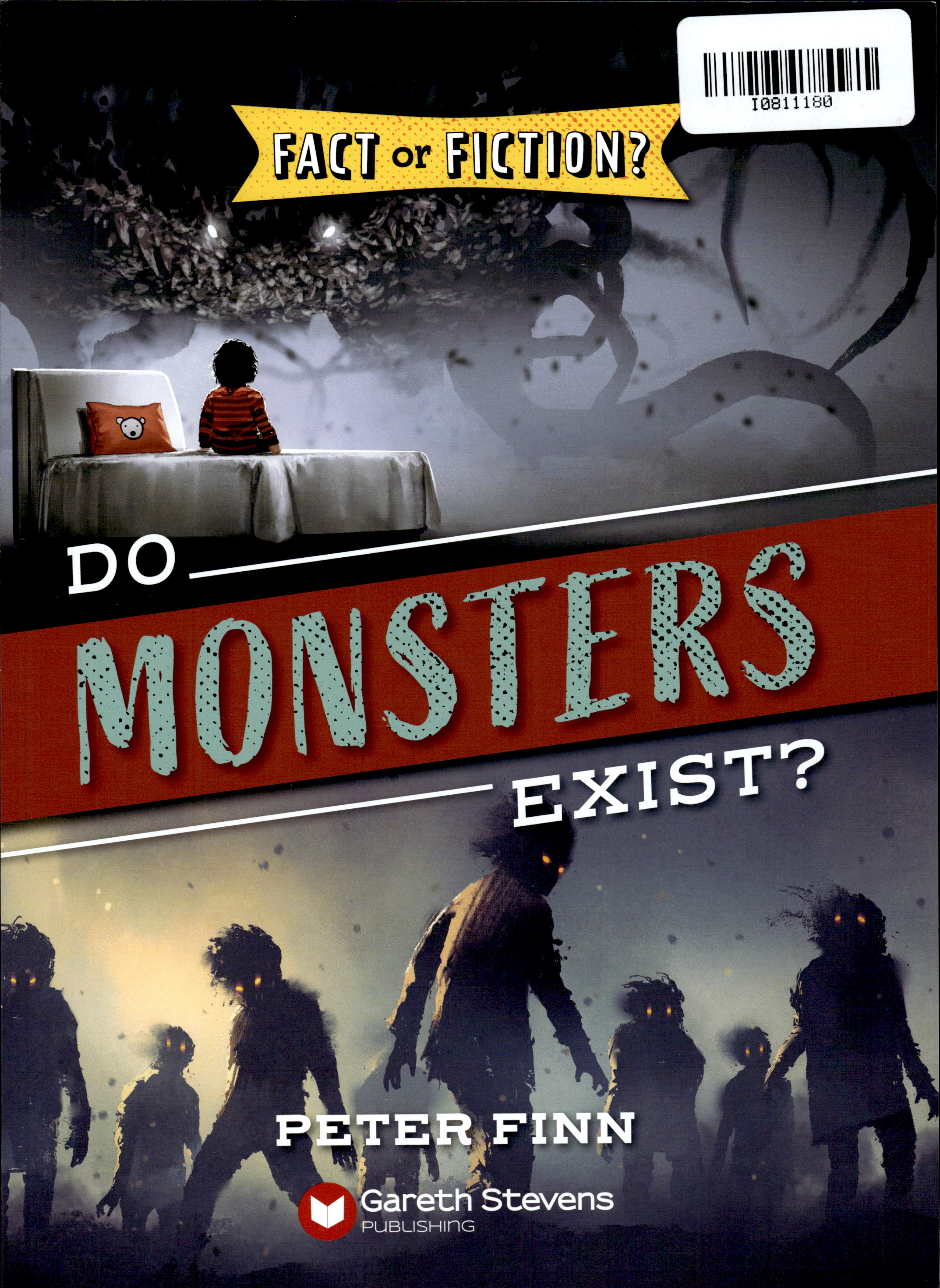

FACT or FICTION?

DO MONSTERS EXIST?

PETER FINN

Gareth Stevens PUBLISHING

Please visit our website, www.garethstevens.com. For a free color catalog of all our high-quality books, call toll free 1-800-542-2595 or fax 1-877-542-2596.

Library of Congress Cataloging-in-Publication Data
Names: Finn, Peter, 1978- author.
Title: Do monsters exist? / Peter Finn.
Description: New York : Gareth Stevens Publishing, 2023. | Series: Fact or fiction? | Includes index.
Identifiers: LCCN 2021058313 (print) | LCCN 2021058314 (ebook) | ISBN 9781538280850 (library binding) | ISBN 9781538280836 (paperback) | ISBN 9781538280843 (set) | ISBN 9781538280867 (ebook)
Subjects: LCSH: Monsters–Juvenile literature. | Animals, Mythical–Juvenile literature.
Classification: LCC GR825 .F56 2023 (print) | LCC GR825 (ebook) | DDC 001.944–dc23/eng/20211214
LC record available at https://lccn.loc.gov/2021058313
LC ebook record available at https://lccn.loc.gov/2021058314

First Edition

Published in 2023 by
Gareth Stevens Publishing
29 E. 21st Street
New York, NY 10010

Designer: Sheryl Kober
Editor: Therese Shea

Photo credits: Cover (top) and p. 1 Tithi Luadthong/Shutterstock.com; cover and p. 1 (bottom image) Tithi Luadthong/Shutterstock.com; pp. 1–32 (background texture) Stephanie Frey/Shutterstock.com; pp. 1–32 (sidebar background texture) welburnstuart/Shutterstock.com; back cover and pp. 2–32 (It's A Fact background texture) Lynn A. Nymeyer/Shutterstock.com; p. 3 Mykhailo Skop/Shutterstock.com; p. 4 Vera Petruk/Shutterstock.com; p. 5 (top) andryuha1981/Shutterstock.com; p. 5 (bottom) https://en.wikipedia.org/wiki/Manticore#/media/File:William_Hastings,_1st_Baron_Hastings.jpeg; p. 6 Alexander_P/Shutterstock.com; p. 7 (top) Daniel Eskridge/Shutterstock.com; p. 7 (bottom) dezignor/Shutterstock.com; p. 8 German Vizulis/Shutterstock.com; p. 9 (top) Willrow Hood/Shutterstock.com; p. 9 (middle) https://commons.wikimedia.org/wiki/File:Poster_-_Frankenstein_02.jpg; p. 9 (bottom) Claudia Longo/Shutterstock.com; p. 10 Svetlana Kurkalova/Shutterstock.com; p. 11 (top) Art disain/Shutterstock.com; p. 11 (bottom left) Refluo/Shutterstock.com; p. 11 (bottom right) FOTOKITA/Shutterstock.com; p. 12 Morphart Creation/Shutterstock.com; p. 13 (top) Natali Strelnik/Shutterstock.com; p. 13 (bottom) Gabi8o/Shutterstock.com; p. 14 (top) Kamaronsky/Shutterstock.com; p 14 (bottom) alya_haciyeva/Shutterstock.com; p. 15 (top) Warpaint/Shutterstock.com; p. 15 (top) Macrovector/Shutterstock.com; p. 16 (bottom) Roselynne/Shutterstock.com; p. 16 (bottom) IADA/Shutterstock.com; p. 17 (top) Daniel Eskridge/Shutterstock.com; p. 17 (bottom) Paul Fleet/Shutterstock.com; p. 18 https://en.wikipedia.org/wiki/Bunyip#/media/File:Bunyip_1890.jpg; p. 19 (top) https://en.wikipedia.org/wiki/Oarfish#/media/File:Giant_Oarfish.jpg; p. 19 (middle) https://en.wikipedia.org/wiki/Kappa_(folklore)#/media/File:Kappastatues.JPG; p. 19 (bottom) https://en.wikipedia.org/wiki/Bunyip#/media/File:Bunyip_(1935).jpg; p. 20 alison1414/Shutterstock.com; p. 21 (top) Daniel Eskridge/Shutterstock.com; p. 21 (bottom) Morphart Creation/Shutterstock.com; p. 22 Vector Tradition/Shutterstock.com; p. 23 (top) Kolonko/Shutterstock.com; p. 23 (loch ness monster icons) Created by Icons Producer from Noun Project; p. 23 (bottom) dnaveh/Shutterstock.com; p. 24 delcamat/Shutterstock.com; p. 25 (in chart from top to bottom) dnaveh/Shutterstock.com, Aldtiya Rakasiwi/Shutterstock.com, Evgery Turaev/Shutterstock.com; HelenField/Shutterstock.com, Jolygon/Shutterstock.com, Paul Fleet/Shutterstock.com, Maquiladora/Shutterstock.com, Ekaterina Gerasimchuk/Shutterstock.com, https://en.wikipedia.org/wiki/Dingiso#/media/File:Dendrolagus_mbaiso.jpg, p. 26 (Top) Larry_Rains/Shutterstock.com; p. 26 (bottom) CPYStudio/Shutterstock.com; p. 27 (top) nRikoBest/Shutterstck.com; p. 27 (bottom) Magnus Linner/Shutterstock.com; p. 28 Daniel Eskridge/Shutterstock.com; p. 29 (top) sevenmaps/Shutterstock.com; p. 29 (bottom) https://en.wikipedia.org/wiki/Mokele-mbembe#/media/File:Mokele-mbembe_ill_artlibre_jnl.png

Printed in the United States of America

CPSIA compliance information: Batch #CSGS23: For further information contact Gareth Stevens, New York, New York, at 1-800-542-2595.

CONTENTS

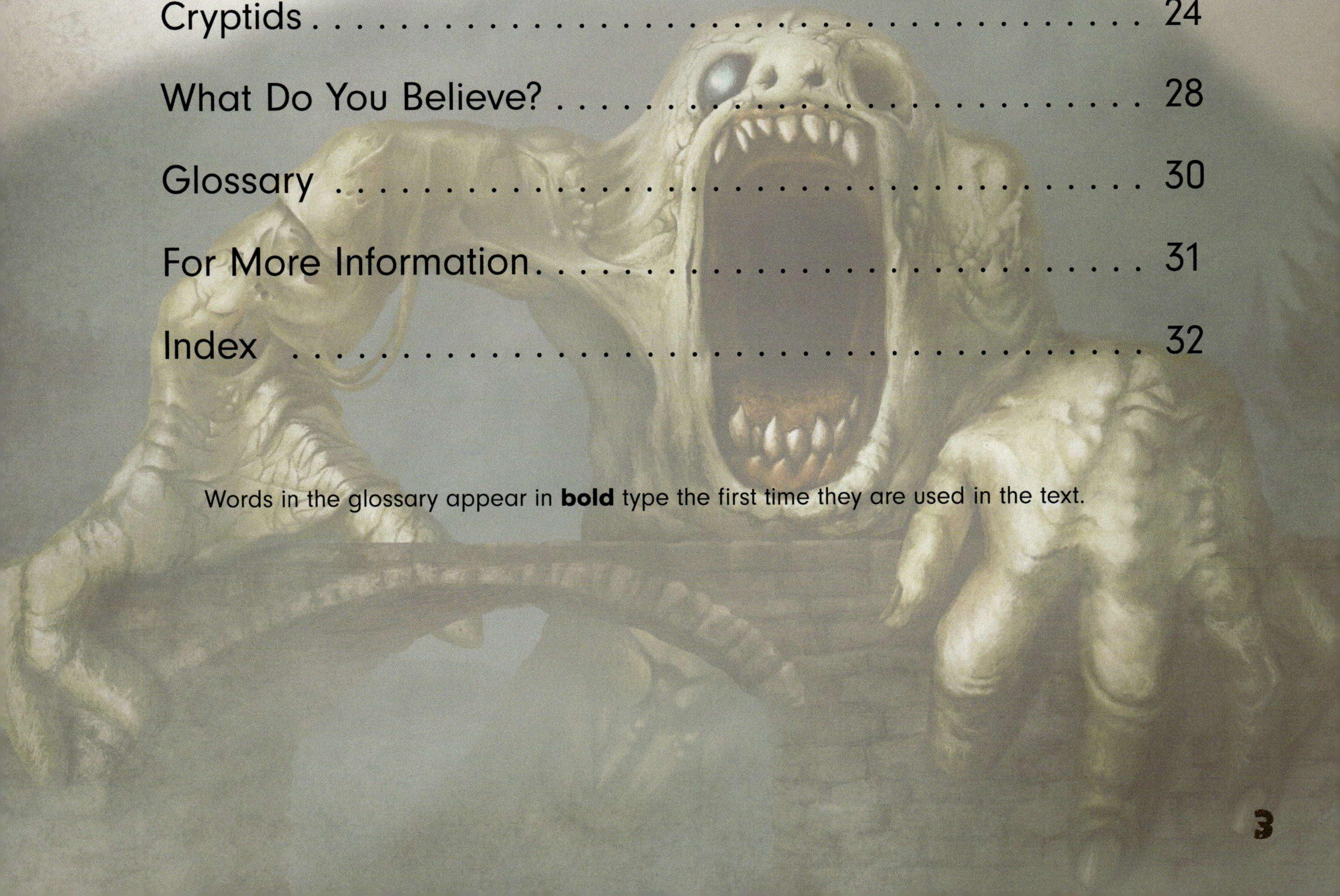

Words in the glossary appear in **bold** type the first time they are used in the text.

SO MANY MONSTERS

The dark of night can seem mysterious and sometimes scary. This is often when imaginations awaken. People may picture something threatening around the next bend on a strange road, in the shadowy figures in a forest, and in the corners underneath their bed—something threatening like a monster!

When you imagine a monster, what do you see? Every person who answers this question answers it differently. Perhaps you picture a hairy beast with sharp claws or a three-headed reptile with glowing red eyes. Maybe it's a huge bug with wings and teeth, or even something invisible!

People around the world tell stories about monsters of all shapes and sizes, as they've been doing for thousands of years. Tales of monsters are exciting, frightening, and sometimes funny. But are any true? Let's investigate.

THE WINDIGO

In this book, you'll learn about monsters in tales from many parts of the world. In North America, the windigo (or wendigo) is a human-eating creature in tales of **Indigenous** peoples, especially those who speak the Algonquian languages, including the Abenaki, Algonquin, and Ojibwe peoples. Many stories about monsters don't have a deeper meaning, but windigo tales warn people not to be greedy, or they may turn into these nasty creatures.

Some legendary monsters are made up of parts from different kinds of animals. A manticore, shown right, has a human head, a lion's body, and a dragon or scorpion's poisonous tail. You can see deer antlers and bear teeth on the statue of the windigo above.

IT'S A FACT!

Legendary beings that are half human and half animal, sometimes called hybrid creatures, are in tales of almost every **culture**.

MONSTERS VS. HEROES

In many Greek myths, terrible monsters threatened people until a brave hero took a stand to face them. The Minotaur had a human body and a bull's head and tail—and ate people. A hero named Theseus killed it.

The Hydra (or Lernaean Hydra) was a snakelike creature with many heads. When one was cut off, two grew in its place. The hero Heracles (Hercules, in Roman myths) destroyed it.

Cerberus was a three-headed dog with sharp fangs that lived in the **underworld** and kept the dead from escaping. The hero Orpheus used music to sneak by Cerberus and into the underworld.

Gorgons were winged women with snakes for hair. The most famous was Medusa. The hero Perseus cut off her head and used it to turn people to stone.

THE MINOTAUR MEETS ITS DOOM

According to legend, the Minotaur was imprisoned in a maze called the labyrinth. At times, the city of Athens was forced to send in 14 people as food for the monster. One year, a prince named Theseus volunteered to go, intending to kill the Minotaur. A princess told him how to find his way out of the labyrinth, by leaving a trail of thread behind him as he went in. Theseus did this, killed the Minotaur, and returned home to Athens a hero.

The mythical Minotaur (left) and Cerberus (below) have inspired the imaginations of artists for thousands of years.

IT'S A FACT!

A Greek poet from the seventh century BCE named Hesiod said Cerberus had 50 heads!

FRANKENSTEIN'S MONSTER

Not all monster legends are as old as the Greek myths. Frankenstein's monster is perhaps one of the most famous monsters in the world. The novel *Frankenstein*: *or, the Modern Prometheus*, by Mary Shelley (pictured at right), was published in 1818. It tells the tale of Victor Frankenstein, a student of science who makes a creature from parts of dead human bodies. He brings his creation to life, but horrified by it, he rejects it. The angry monster kills several people in Frankenstein's life, causing the scientist great sadness. Frankenstein chases his monster into the Arctic, where the scientist dies. The monster weeps over his creator's body and wanders away to die too.

This story inspired many movies and writings. Likely the most famous is a 1931 film called *Frankenstein*, in which actor Boris Karloff plays the monster.

MORE TO KNOW ABOUT FRANKENSTEIN

People often think "Frankenstein" is the name of the monster in Mary Shelley's book, but it's the name of the scientist who created him—Victor Frankenstein. The monster himself is never given a name in the novel, though he compares himself to Adam in the Bible. People also think of the monster as a creature that grunts and moans, as he did in movies. In Mary Shelley's book, however, the creature is intelligent and well spoken.

The 1931 *Frankenstein* movie created the monster's look, which has lasted in popular culture.

IT'S A FACT!

Mary Shelley's book was published without an author's name at first. Her name was added in 1831.

WEREWOLVES

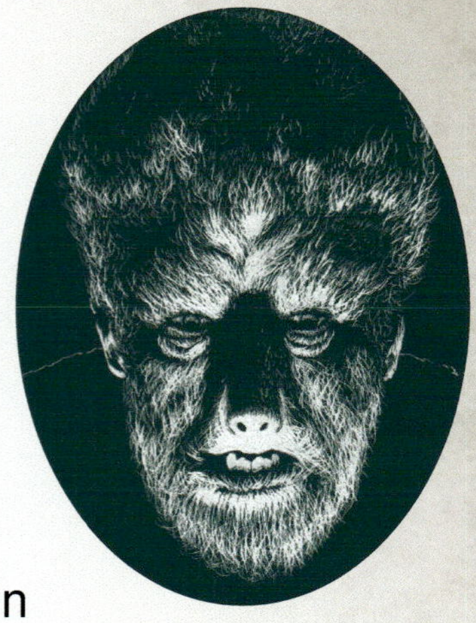

Some think werewolf folklore goes back to prehistoric times. Werewolves were a part of Greek and Roman mythology as well. In **medieval** times in Europe, werewolf tales were passed on as truth, supported by the fact that some people dressed as wolves to scare others! These tales were told especially in places where wolves were plentiful and a dangerous problem for the people living nearby.

According to some stories, werewolves are people who transform into powerful, bloodthirsty wolves, often when the moon is full. Others say werewolves are part human and part wolf. No matter what form, they tend to be hungry killers.

Many stories suggest a person becomes a werewolf after being bitten by a werewolf. Other lore says a person who drinks rainwater from a wolf's footprint may become a werewolf.

LYCANTHROPY

Lycanthropy is a rare mental health disorder in which someone believes they're an animal rather than a human being. The kind of animal is often linked to the dangerous predators that live near the person who has lycanthropy. That could be a wolf in Europe, a leopard in Africa, or a tiger in China, for example. The word "lycanthropy" comes from the Greek words *lykos* (wolf) and *anthropos* (man).

Some stories say werewolves turn into vampires after death.

IT'S A FACT!

Hypertrichosis is a condition in which an unusual amount of hair grows on a person's body. Long ago, those with hypertrichosis were likely thought to be werewolves.

VAMPIRES

Another common monster in stories is the vampire. Vampires in different tales have different features and behaviors. Most vampires are said to drink human blood, often through their special fangs. They're also described as "undead," meaning their human bodies died but rose again. Some stories tell of vampires needing to sleep in coffins during the day and hunting at night. Like the werewolf, stories of this creature come from many places, including China, the Philippines, North America, and Europe.

The most famous vampire story, *Dracula*, takes place partly in Transylvania, a region in modern-day Romania. Written in 1897 by Irish author Bram Stoker, *Dracula* is the tale of the undead Count Dracula, who feeds off the blood of the living.

REAL-LIFE DRACULA

It seems pretty unbelievable, but Bram Stoker partly based his character on a real person from history, Vlad III Dracula. Vlad was a prince in Walachia, a region in Transylvania, during the 15th century. He was known for shocking cruelty to his enemies, **impaling** their bodies on stakes, for example. For that, he's sometimes called Vlad the Impaler. Stoker doesn't include these details in his book, but borrowed Vlad's name, Dracula, which means "son of Dracul," for his frighteningly evil main character.

Bran Castle (above) in Romania is sometimes known as Dracula's Castle. Bram Stoker may have been inspired by a likeness he saw of this castle before writing his book.

Vlad III Dracula (at right).

IT'S A FACT!

While vampire legends existed long before Bram Stoker's novel, many qualities of vampires in stories that followed are based on his book.

Long ago, stories about vampires were told to explain illness and death. For example, medieval people who died of plague sometimes had blood around their mouths. This looked to some like they had been drinking blood. It was also said that vampires couldn't be in sunlight. People who had conditions that made it difficult for them to be in the sun could be suspected of vampirism too. Similar suspicions fell on people with other physical or mental differences.

Years ago, people didn't understand that diseases can spread through **infection**. They sometimes blamed sicknesses on a vampire in their community. They thought killing the suspected vampire could save lives. Sometimes this meant digging up a dead body and plunging a stake through its heart!

EVIDENCE OF FEAR

People have been worrying about vampires as recently as the 1830s in New England. In 1990, a grave in Griswold, Connecticut, was uncovered in which the remains of a man were strangely arranged: the skull had been taken off, and the ribs were broken, as if someone had tried to remove the heart. Historians believe this damage had been done about five years after the man had died. He was likely suspected of being a vampire.

How did people protect themselves from vampires? Garlic, running water, and crosses were among the objects believed to keep them away.

IT'S A FACT!

The three species of bloodsucking vampire bats feed on the blood of animals, not people.

MONSTERS OF THE SEA

Throughout history, people have feared monsters in oceans, seas, lakes, rivers, and other bodies of water. Before modern **technology**, it was hard to explore deep waters. Every seagoing culture had tales about strange aquatic, or water-dwelling, creatures.

The kraken was one of these creatures. It seems to have come from **Scandinavian** folklore. Its description matches that of an extremely large octopus or squid. Its body was said to be about 1.5 miles (2.4 km) around, and its arms could be mistaken for islands!

The kraken was thought to live near Iceland and Norway, where it ate mainly fish. It didn't try to harm ships or eat sailors. However, if a boat sailed too close, the kraken's incredible size was said to cause the vessel to turn over or get pulled under the water.

REAL-LIFE SEA MONSTER

Scientists think they've solved the mystery of the kraken legend. Tales of the kraken may come from sightings of the giant squid. While these ocean creatures have washed up dead on shore over the years, they've been hard to observe alive in the ocean. In 2004, Japanese scientists finally captured images of this "monster" in the North Pacific Ocean. In 2012, a giant squid was recorded using a video camera.

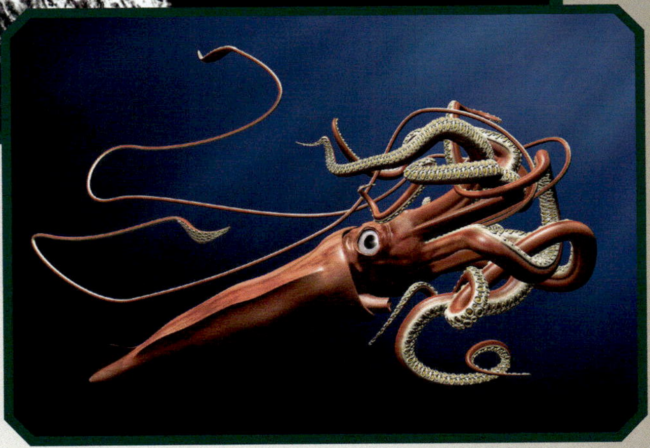

The giant squid isn't as large as the kraken of legends, but it's still impressive. The largest adults can be nearly 60 feet (18 m) in length.

IT'S A FACT!

The kraken story dates back to around 1180 CE.

The kraken isn't the only aquatic monster of folklore by far. In Japanese tales, the *kappa* looked like a yellowish-green monkey with a turtle shell or fish scales, depending on the legend. It tries to pull people into the water, but is said to love to eat cucumbers!

Aboriginal Australians, the earliest peoples on the continent, tell stories of the bunyip, a type of swamp monster that feeds on women and children. It was described with various body parts, sometimes like a human and sometimes like a **manatee**, hippopotamus, or ox, but with long, sharp tusks. Some said the bunyip had fur, while others said scales or feathers. It made frightening noises described as roaring or booming. Bunyip tales changed with the arrival of Europeans in Australia, making the creature more harmless.

OTHER EXPLANATIONS

Many kinds of water animals can look unusual and even monstrous, especially if seen in the distance or at night. Maybe sailors really saw crocodiles, octopuses, squid, sea turtles, sharks, or whales when they told others of monster sightings. The oarfish (page 19, top image) is an especially long, strange-looking fish that looks a lot like a monster to some. An oarfish can grow to be 30.5 feet (9.3 m) long. It certainly could have inspired **sea serpent** legends.

Tales of the bunyip (below) may come from rare sightings of seals swimming upriver into Australia.

Kappa (above).

IT'S A FACT!

The colossal squid was first identified in 1925. Its eyes are likely the largest of all animals, about 9.8 inches (25 cm) across!

LAKE MONSTER LEGENDS

Just as sailors told sea monster stories, people who live near lakes may tell stories of lake monsters. Probably the most famous lake monster is "Nessie," the Loch Ness monster. Loch Ness is in the Highlands of Scotland and is the largest freshwater source by volume in Great Britain. The loch, or lake, is 23 miles (37 km) long and around 788 feet (240 m) at its deepest point.

Over 1,500 years ago, a northern Scottish people called the Picts carved creatures in stone, including an elephant-like animal with flippers. Some believe this is the oldest evidence of the Loch Ness monster. The lore has only grown over the years, and many people have said they've seen the creature. From the descriptions most give, some claim Nessie is a plesiosaur.

THE LAST OF THE PLESIOSAURS?

A plesiosaur is a type of marine reptile believed to have become extinct about 66 million years ago. However, some think plesiosaurs have somehow survived in Loch Ness. Others think it's more likely that witnesses have seen large waves or large fish, such as sturgeon or catfish. While most photographs are proven to be hoaxes or unconvincing at best, people keep looking for Nessie. Scientists have even used underwater submarines and **sonar** in their searches.

Is Loch Ness big enough and deep enough to hide a real monster?

IT'S A FACT!

Perhaps the most famous Loch Ness monster photograph turned out to be a fake. The "monster" was a model head attached to a toy submarine.

North America has lake monster legends too. Champ is the name of the creature said to live in Lake Champlain, which borders the U.S. states of Vermont and New York and flows into the Canadian province of Quebec. A creature called Ogopogo is said to hide in the waters of Okanagan Lake of British Columbia. The Syilx Okanagan People who live in the region have long told of the lake's sacred spirit—not monster—which they call *n'x̌ax̌aitk*^{w} (n-ha-ha-it-koo).

The Lakota and Dakota peoples have legends of the Unktehila (oonk-tay-hee-lah), a horned water serpent. Similar creatures appear in the lore of the Cherokee, Ojibwe, Cheyenne, and Passamaquoddy peoples. Sometimes these beings and others are ways to explain natural events, disappearances, and deaths in a body of water.

POSSIBILITIES

What could be in these bodies of water if not monsters? A study of Loch Ness revealed the lake has many eels. An especially big eel might fool someone who's on the lookout for Nessie. Large waves are another explanation. According to scientist Robert Young who studied Okanagan Lake, waves can occur when a **dense** layer of water slides under a less dense layer of water, pushing up on it. Oddly shaped logs can also trick the eye.

LAKE MONSTERS of the UNITED STATES of AMERICA

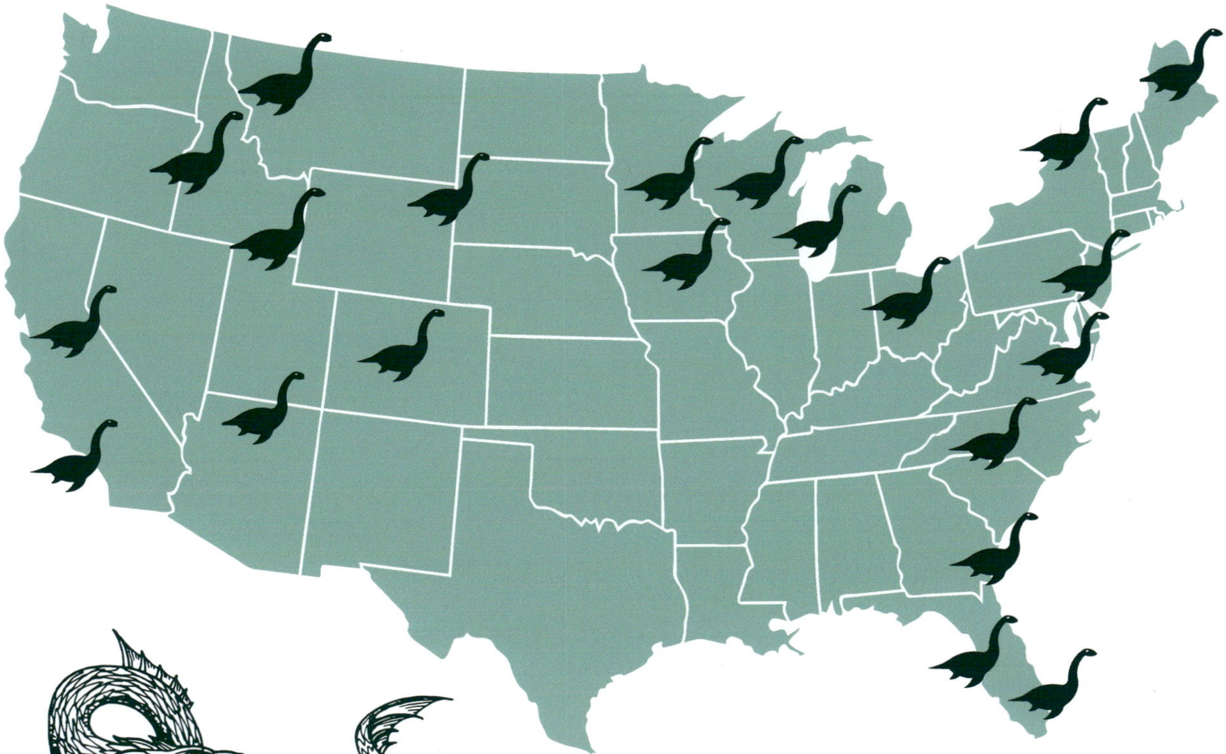

According to the website Atlas Obscura, these are the locations of sightings of Nessie-like lake monsters in the United States.

Can you see yourself mistaking this wave for a lake monster?

IT'S A FACT!

Lake monsters are good for tourism. Nessie is thought to bring over $50 million a year to Scotland's economy.

CRYPTIDS

A cryptid is an animal whose existence has been suggested but never proven. Cryptids are often said to live in oceans, forests, or mountains—all places out of the way of most humans. Monster lore is full of cryptids.

The *chupacabra* (which means "goat sucker" in Spanish) is a creature that supposedly lives in the Americas and survives by drinking the blood of livestock and other animals. It's been described as about the size of a large dog with red eyes and a row of spikes from its neck down the length of its back. The so-called Jersey Devil is another cryptid. It's reported to be kangaroo-like with a horse's face, horns, bat-like wings, and a tail. It's been blamed for the deaths of animals in New Jersey.

THE DEATH WORM!

The Gobi is a desert in Central Asia. According to some, it's also the home of another cryptid: the Mongolian Death Worm. It's described as red in color and not too large, about 3 feet (0.9 m) long, with spikes on both ends. However, the wormlike creature is said to be able to spit a deadly toxin. If it doesn't hit its victim, it supposedly can kill it with a jolt of electricity—from a distance!

From Questionable Cryptids to Actual Animals

1802 platypus

1847 gorilla

1869 giant panda

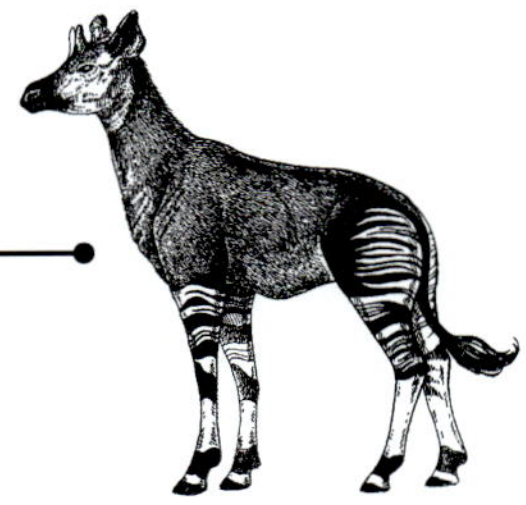

1901 okapi

1912 Komodo dragon

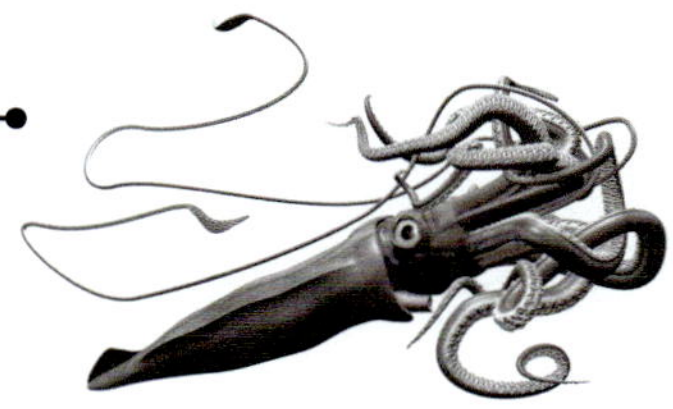

1925 colossal squid

1976 megamouth shark

1984 giant gecko

1994 dingiso (bondegezou)

It may surprise you how recently some of these animals were proven to be real in the scientific community.

IT'S A FACT!

As much as $100,000 has been offered for the capture of the Jersey Devil. However, no one's ever caught it.

Perhaps the most famous cryptid in North America is Bigfoot. This beast (or beasts!) may roam the forests of the northwestern United States and western Canada. Many people say they've seen huge footprints, strange hairs, or even Bigfoot itself. They claim it's a huge apelike creature, much taller and hairier than a human. The Salish people of the area call this legendary figure Sasquatch, from the Salish word *se'sxac* (wild men).

Some think there's an ancient answer to the Bigfoot mystery. *Gigantopithecus* was a large ape that existed in southern China until about 11,700 years ago. The creature is a distant relative to the modern orangutan and stood nearly 10 feet (3 m) tall. Could this ape have ended up in the Pacific Northwest—and survived all this time?

YETI AND FRIENDS

In the Himalayas, the yeti is a creature similar to Sasquatch but white to match the snowy mountains. People of the region tell stories of the yeti, also called the abominable snowman. The yeti isn't spotted much, but large footprints are often used as evidence of its existence. Some think bears cause these marks by walking a certain way, combining their front and back pawprints to create one set of very large footprints.

Skeptics think the hair and footprints thought by some to belong to Sasquatch, or Bigfoot, are from bears or other animals. Scientists can test the DNA of hair and skin to match it to known animals' DNA.

IT'S A FACT!

Other cultures tell stories of legendary snow creatures too, such as Nee-gued in India and Almas in Central Asia.

WHAT DO YOU BELIEVE?

This book couldn't possibly include *all* monsters of folklore. If you can't get enough of monster tales, keep reading and researching in other books. You might want to learn about the Mokele-mbembe of the African Congo. It's said to be an elephant-size plant eater that looks like a long-necked dinosaur. Or maybe the rakshasas of Hindu myths are more interesting to you. These demons were said to be able to change shape.

While books and movies feature plenty of monsters, do you think any could exist outside the stories? Remember, there are parts of Earth that aren't well explored, and scientists are finding new species regularly. Next time you hear an unexplained noise or see a curious shadow, ask yourself: Could it be a monster?

LOCAL MONSTERS

You may have some monster lore in your community. For example, there are reports of a giant freshwater octopus in Oklahoma's Lake Thunderbird and a half man, half goat in a lake near Fort Worth, Texas. People near Lake Erie have said they spied a sea serpent they named South Bay Bessie. The monster legend near you may live in the woods, a field, or anywhere else. Check your nearest library for local monster lore!

Biologist Bill Laurance told BBC News, "My gut sense is that the likelihood of the [Mokele-mbembe] actually existing today is small. However, one thing you learn early on in science is never say never."

IT'S A FACT!

The Congo River basin, where the Mokele-mbembe is said to roam, is about 1.3 million square miles (3.4 million sq km). That's a big place to hide!

GLOSSARY

culture: the beliefs and ways of life of a group of people

dense: having parts that are packed very closely together

impale: to cause a pointed object to go into or through something or someone else

Indigenous: having to do with the first known people to settle in an area

infection: a sickness caused by germs. Also, the spread of germs inside the body, causing illness.

manatee: a large, plant-eating marine mammal that lives in coastal and inland waters. It has paddle-shaped flippers and a flat, rounded tail.

medieval: having to do with the Middle Ages, a time in European history from about 500 to 1500 CE

Scandinavian: from the region of northern Europe called Scandinavia now occupied by Norway, Sweden, and Denmark. Sometimes Scandinavia also includes Iceland and Finland.

sea serpent: a large marine animal said to look like a snake that hasn't been proven to exist

skeptic: someone who has doubt or disbelief about a certain subject

sonar: a machine that uses sound waves to find things in a body of water

technology: using science, engineering, and other industries to invent useful tools or to solve problems. Also a machine, piece of equipment, or method created by technology.

underworld: in mythology, the place where souls go after death

FOR MORE INFORMATION

BOOKS

Karst, Ken. *Sea Monsters*. Mankato, MN: Creative Education, 2020.

Pratt, Laura. *Monsters*. New York, NY: AV2, 2021.

Robertson, K. A. *Monsters.* Vero Beach, FL: Rourke Educational Media, 2019.

WEBSITES

6 Mythical Monsters
www.history.com/news/6-mythical-monsters
Read about these monsters—if you dare!

Freaky Creatures
kids.nationalgeographic.com/videos/topic/freaky-creatures
Learn about real creatures with some freaky monster traits.

Is There Any Proof that Bigfoot Is Real?
wonderopolis.org/wonder/is-there-any-proof-that-bigfoot-is-real
Find out more about Bigfoot and what Bigfoot hunters are up to.

INDEX